To my Mom, Dad & Grandparents, Thank you.

To my beautiful daughters,
Cara, Lauren, & Alyssa ... life is an adventure. I love you!

To my future grandchildren, this is for you.

To my Family & Friends, especially Jim Lorenzo, Our history tells us how we evolved. Let the memory live on generation to generation as we continue the traditions of our immigrant ancestors.

To the many students I have taught, especially at Brighton, Bristol, Lakewood, Randall, Wheatland, and Wilmot Union High School, your interest and enthusiasm in my books always made me smile. I hope they inspire you to take action and make your dreams come true.

To the Ellis Island Archives in New York and the Melrose Park Public Library in Illinois. Thank you. Your expertise is appreciated after weeks of research.

Balboa Press books may be ordered through booksellers or by contacting:

Balboa Press
A Division of Hay House
1663 Liberty Drive
Bloomington, IN 47403
www.balboapress.com
1 (877) 407-4847

ISBN: 978-1-9822-2337-3 (sc)
ISBN: 978-1-9822-2336-6 (e)

Library of Congress Control Number: 2019902825

Print information available on the last page.

Balboa Press rev. date: 05/09/2019

BALBOA
PRESS
A DIVISION OF HAY HOUSE

A Journal

A Recipe &

A Family in America

Nora Rose

My Great Uncle Saverio Iovino grew up in Naples, Italy. When he was a boy he planted cucumbers, tomatoes, and green peppers with his family. He took extra care of the peach tree because he liked to eat this sweet, juicy fruit.

1

He remembered the promise his brother Gabriel made with him about moving to America. In 1925, at age 17, Saverio sailed on a ship to the United States in search of new opportunities. His two sisters hugged him and said, "We believe in you. It doesn't matter how difficult it gets, believe it's possible." They wrote this down for him to keep in his pocket.

"Find work but take time to write," his father said, handing him a journal.

"Live in happiness." "And always remember your family," said his mother. She hugged him, gave him a picture and her recipe for pizza.

It was an intense 16 day voyage across the ocean on the S.S.Dante Alighieri. Saverio passed the time by playing cards with others on the ship.

Every night he read the note. "We believe in you. It doesn't matter how difficult it gets, believe it's possible." He wrote the one hundred successes of his life in his journal and waited for the ship to land.

The Dante Alighieri

The big buildings of America were different from his small Italian town. *Greetings* from the Statue of Liberty represented a new feeling of freedom. He didn't know it at the time but like many immigrants coming to America he would take another name. Saverio Iovino was now Sam Iovino. He was happy to start his new life. He was healthy and able to contribute to this new country.

After he passed inspection in New York he boarded a train to Chicago. His brother was married to Phyllis and welcomed him into their home. There were many Italians helping each other in this new city. Gabriel found work for Sam as a laborer doing construction on the transportation system known as the Chicago Subway. Every night Sam wrote in his journal and added to his one hundred successes in life.

Sam met Carmela, and soon they were married. They had five daughters and did their best to teach them to believe it's possible, live happiness, write in their journals, remember their family and celebrate traditions. He told them how pizza originated in Italy.

In 1889, on their visit to Naples, King Umberto and Queen Margherita had a pizza created for them. "The Margherita" was named after her. Today, it is still the famous fresh tomato, basil and mozzarella cheese pizza we all enjoy!

11

Gabriel's family and Sam's family had Sunday dinners together. Their wives cooked many traditional pasta meals. "A pinch of this" and "a handful of that" was creative, exhilarating, and satisfying to them. The children helped in the kitchen. They watched and learned that preparing a meal was an art, mixed with science and experimentation and just the right amount of love. Cooking was the thread that connected people and places to family, history, religion and tradition. The tempting smells were delicious and they loved to eat. The dinner table looked like a masterpiece.

Gabriel had always dreamed of a cottage in the country. He took a long ride to Wisconsin, believed it was possible, and bought land just as he had imagined. He, his wife and five children worked hard to build a house by a lake with a big yard and celebrated family there. They named one of their daughters Carmella. She is my mother.

On summer days Sam would drive his family to the country to visit with Gabriel. The children would spend the weekend playing softball, fishing or reading books.

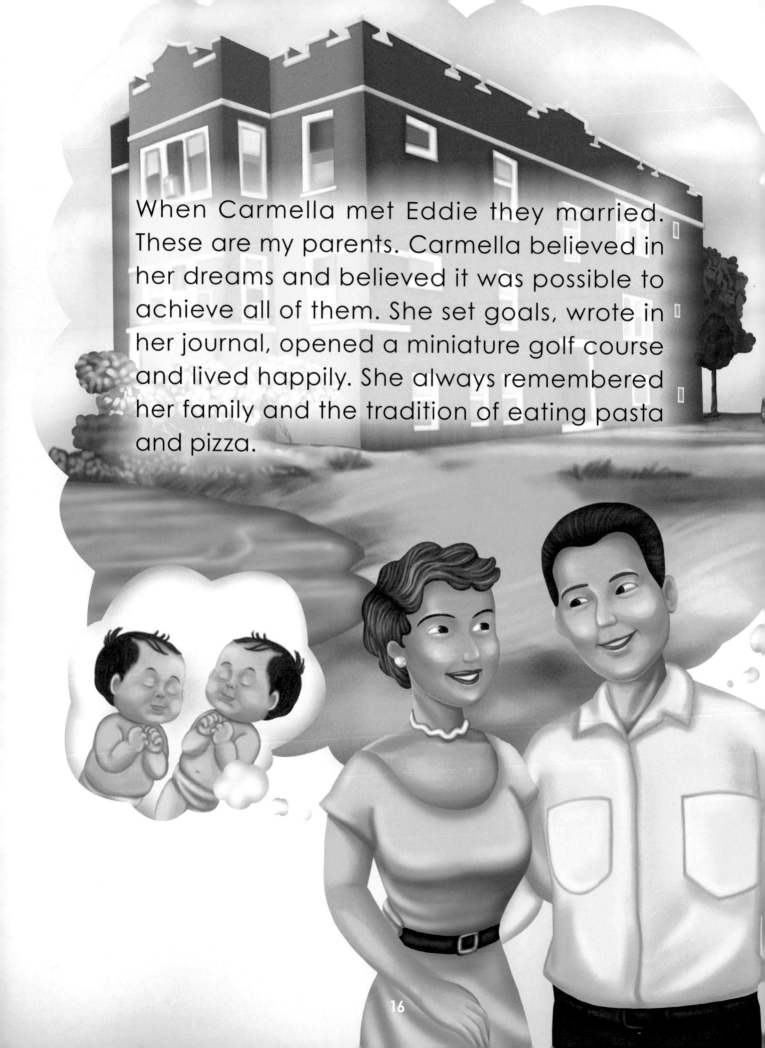

When Carmella met Eddie they married. These are my parents. Carmella believed in her dreams and believed it was possible to achieve all of them. She set goals, wrote in her journal, opened a miniature golf course and lived happily. She always remembered her family and the tradition of eating pasta and pizza.

My sister and I grew up next door to my grandparents, Gabriel and Phyllis in Chicago. We also took long rides to the country staying at the cottage. I would walk through the garden picking the tomatoes, cucumbers, apples, grapes and flowers. But mostly, we would spend all day swimming at the beach.

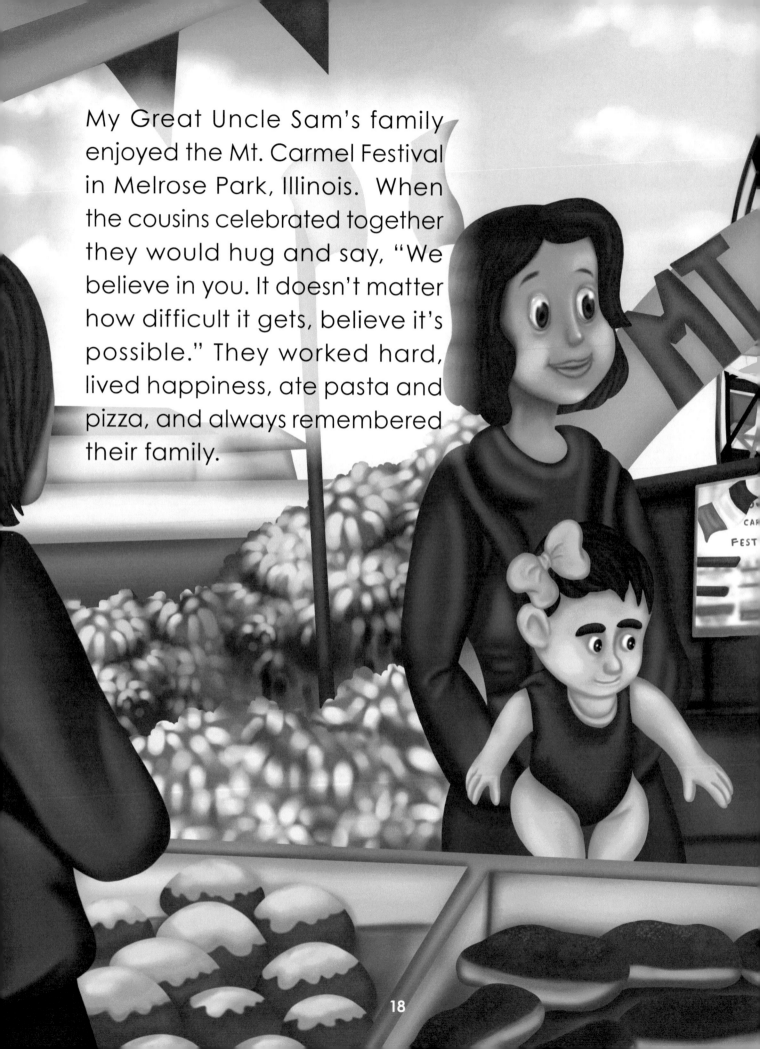

My Great Uncle Sam's family enjoyed the Mt. Carmel Festival in Melrose Park, Illinois. When the cousins celebrated together they would hug and say, "We believe in you. It doesn't matter how difficult it gets, believe it's possible." They worked hard, lived happiness, ate pasta and pizza, and always remembered their family.

My father handed me a journal, "Believe in your dreams and live happiness," he said. "Remember your family," said my mother. I wrote goals in my journal and believed that I would achieve all of them.

When I got married I had three daughters. I taught my children to believe in their dreams, write goals in their journals, live happiness and remember their family. We celebrated family traditions, ate pasta and pizza, grew basil and tomatoes in our garden and visited Naples, Italy. We are grateful for the life we live.

So I remind you dear reader, believe in your dreams, write goals in your journal, work hard to achieve them, write the one hundred successes of your life, live happiness, remember your family and celebrate traditions.

22

"A goal is a dream with a deadline." ~ Napoleon Hill

A Journal

Journal writing can help you clear your head and make important connections between thoughts, feelings, behaviors and experiences. Journal writing is good to establish future goals, problem solve, improve writing skills, recall memories, personal growth, and spark inner creativity. Studies show journaling can also improve memory and lower stress levels.

Is it worth writing a goal down? Yes, it is. You have a 42% higher chance of reaching your goal when you start writing it down. You give it a name, a deadline and a description to see how much farther you have to go to take action to achieve it.

According to a study conducted by Dr. Gail Matthews, a psychology professor at Dominican University of California, you are 42% more likely to achieve your goals just by writing them down.

Did you know having a goal can make you happier? When you write down your goal you commit to something bigger and better than what you have now and that gives you hope. Just like Sam, Gabriel and Carmella in the story. Hope for a better tomorrow, hope for a better future, hope that the happiness you seek can actually be achieved.

The most important part of writing down your goal is to take action. Proceed with your dream, write it down, take the steps to make it come true.

In this story Sam wrote the 100 Successes List to increase his self confidence. He was thinking of all the things he accomplished in his life up to now and kept adding more as he began his journey of a lifetime. Try it. Did you learn to ride a bike, drive a car, graduate 8th grade, high school, or college, or get married? YOU have more successes than you realize. Go on, you can do it. Write them down and keep adding to your list. YOU are successful!

A Recipe for Margherita Pizza

Ingredients:

* Pizza dough - make your own, buy dough, or use cauliflower pizza crust
* 1 Tablespoon olive oil
* 2 cloves roasted garlic, finely chopped
* 1/4 cup your favorite pizza or tomato sauce
* 8 ounces mozzarella cheese, sliced into 1/2 inch thick pieces
* 2 plum tomatoes, sliced (or any tomato you like)
* Handful of fresh basil
* Fresh ground pepper, to taste

Directions:

1. Prepare pizza dough, preheat the oven to 450°F (246°C). Arrange a rack in the bottom third of the oven. Place a heavy rimmed baking sheet upside-down on the rack, and heat the oven. Cover the shaped dough lightly with plastic wrap and allow it to rest as the oven preheats. If the dough is sticky, dust with a little bit of all-purpose flour. Dust a 12-inch piece of parchment paper with cornmeal and place the dough on it. Use the heel of your hand to press the dough flat. Work from the middle out to shape it into a 10-inch round with your hands or a rolling pin. The dough will stick to the parchment; if it starts to shrink back, wait a few minutes to let it relax and continue shaping. Place on baking sheet.

2. Mix the olive oil and chopped garlic together in a small dish. Brush the top of the dough lightly with olive oil. Using your fingers, push dents into the surface of the dough to prevent bubbling. Top with pizza sauce, then the mozzarella cheese slices, then the tomato slices. Carefully remove the preheated baking sheet from the oven and use the parchment paper to slide the pizza onto the back of the baking sheet.

3. Bake for 14-16 minutes or until the crust is lightly browned and the cheese is bubbling.

4. Remove from the oven. Add the fresh basil and pepper. Slice pizza and serve immediately. **ENJOY** your pizza!! *Buon Appetito!!*

5. Cover leftover pizza tightly and store in the refrigerator. Reheat as you prefer. Baked pizza slices can be frozen up to 3 months.

"If you want to bring happiness to the whole world, go home and love your family." ~ Mother Teresa

A Family In America

A person can spend their entire lives in the United States and never naturalize. Naturalization is a voluntary process.

Saverio Iovino's naturalization papers were found on Ancestry.com in the database entitled, "Illinois Federal Naturalization Records, 1865-1991." These records are in the custody of the National Archives at Chicago. The passenger manifests have been digitalized and are available on Ancestry.com in the database entitled, "New York Passenger Manifests, 1820-1957."

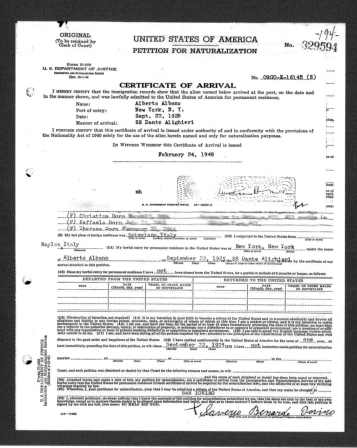

ORIGINAL
(To be retained by
Clerk of Court)

UNITED STATES OF AMERICA

No. 329594

PETITION FOR NATURALIZATION

[Of a Married Person, under Sec. 310(a) or 310(b) or 311 or 312, of the Nationality Act of 1940 (54 Stat. 1144-1145)]

To the Honorable the DISTRICT Court of THE UNITED STATES at CHICAGO, ILLINOIS

This petition for naturalization, hereby made and filed pursuant to Section 310(a) or (b), or Section 311 or 312, of the Nationality Act of 1940, respectively shows:

(1) My full, true, and correct name is SAVERIO BERNARDO IOVINO also known as SAM IOVINO

(2) My present place of residence is 1009 N. 25th Ave., Melrose Park, Ill. My occupation is Welder

(4) I am 39 years old. I was born on August 1, 1908 in Sisciano, Italy

(6) My personal description is as follows: Sex male; color white; complexion fair, color of eyes grey, color of hair black, height 5 feet 4 inches, weight 135 pounds; visible distinctive marks none; race white; present nationality Italian

(7) I am married; the name of my wife or husband is Carmela; we were married on September 6, 1930 at Chicago, Illinois; he or she was born at Chicago, Illinois on May 30, 1911

entered the United States at for permanent residence in the United States, and now resides at Melrose Park, Ill. and was naturalized on at certificate No. or became a citizen by birth

(7a) [If petition is filed under Section 311, Nationality Act of 1940] I have resided in the United States in marital union with my United States citizen spouse for at least 1 year immediately preceding the date of filing this petition for naturalization.

(8) I have four children; and the name, sex, date and place of birth, and present place of residence of each of said children who is living, are as follows:

(F) Rose Born
(F) Christina Born
(F) Raffaela Born
(F) Theresa Born

(9) My last place of foreign residence was Sisciano, Italy (10) I emigrated to the United States from Naples Italy (11) My lawful entry for permanent residence in the United States was at New York, New York under the name of Alberto Albano on September 22, 1925 on the SS Dante Alighieri by the certificate of my arrival attached to this petition.

(12) Since my lawful entry for permanent residence I have not been absent from the United States, for a period or periods of 6 months or longer, as follows:

DEPARTED FROM THE UNITED STATES			RETURNED TO THE UNITED STATES		
PORT	DATE (Month, day, year)	VESSEL OR OTHER MEANS OF CONVEYANCE	PORT	DATE (Month, day, year)	VESSEL OR OTHER MEANS OF CONVEYANCE

(13) (Declaration of intention not required) (14) It is my intention in good faith to become a citizen of the United States and to renounce absolutely and forever all allegiance and fidelity to any foreign prince, potentate, state, or sovereignty of whom or which at this time I am a subject or citizen, and it is my intention to reside permanently in the United States. (15) I am not, and have not been for the period of at least 10 years immediately preceding the date of this petition, an anarchist; nor a believer in the unlawful damage, injury, or destruction of property, or sabotage; nor a disbeliever in or opposed to organized government; nor a member of or affiliated with any organization or body of persons teaching disbelief in or opposition to organized government. (16) I am able to speak the English language (unless physically unable to do so). (17) I am, and have been during all of the periods required by law, attached to the principles of the Constitution of the United States and well disposed to the good order and happiness of the United States. (18) I have resided continuously in the United States of America for the term of one year at least immediately preceding the date of this petition, to wit: since September 22, 1925 (19) I have not heretofore made petition for naturalization

number on at (City or town) (County) (State) in the (Name of court)

Court, and such petition was dismissed or denied by that Court for the following reasons and causes, to wit: and the cause of such dismissal or denial has since been cured or removed.

(20) Attached hereto and made a part of this, my petition for naturalization, are a certificate of arrival from the Immigration and Naturalization Service of my said lawful entry into the United States for permanent residence (if such certificate of arrival is required by the naturalization law), and the affidavit of at least two verifying witnesses required by law.

(21) Wherefore, I, your petitioner for naturalization, pray that I may be admitted a citizen of the United States of America, and that my name be changed to SAM IOVINO

(22) I, aforesaid petitioner, do swear (affirm) that I know the contents of this petition for naturalization subscribed by me, that the same are true to the best of my own knowledge, except as to matters therein stated to be alleged upon information and belief, and that as to those matters I believe them to be true, and that this petition is signed by me with my full, true name: SO HELP ME GOD.

Saverio Bernardo Iovino
(Full, true, and correct signature of petitioner, without abbreviation)

AFFIDAVIT OF WITNESSES

The following witnesses, each being severally, duly, and respectively sworn, depose and say:

My name is Tony Bonavalonta my occupation is Insurance Man
I reside at 1009 N. 25th Avenue, Melrose Park, Ill.

My name is Dominick Serpico my occupation is Retired
I reside at 917 N. 23rd Avenue, Melrose Park, Ill.

I am a citizen of the United States of America; I have personally known and have been acquainted in the United States with Saverio Bernardo Iovino known as Sam Iovino, the petitioner named in the petition for naturalization of which this affidavit is a part, since July 1, 1940 to my personal knowledge the petitioner has resided, immediately preceding the date of filing this petition, in the United States continuously since the date last mentioned, and I have personal knowledge that the petitioner is now and during all such period has been a person of good moral character, attached to the principles of the Constitution of the United States, and well disposed to the good order and happiness of the United States, and in my opinion the petitioner is in every way qualified to be admitted a citizen of the United States.

I do swear (affirm) that the statements of fact I have made in this affidavit of this petition for naturalization subscribed by me are true to the best of my knowledge and belief: SO HELP ME GOD.

Dominick Serpico   Tony Bonavalonta
(Signature of witness)   (Signature of witness)

Subscribed and sworn to before me by the above-named petitioner and witnesses, in the respective forms of oath shown in said petition and affidavit, in the office of the Clerk of said Court at Chicago, Illinois, this 25th day of March Anno Domini 1948 I hereby certify that Certificate of Arrival No. 0900-K-16145 (S) from the Immigration and Naturalization Service, showing the lawful entry for permanent residence of the petitioner above named, has been by me filed with, attached to, and made a part of this petition on this date.

ROY H. JOHNSON, Clerk.

H N

By [illegible] Deputy Clerk. [SEAL]

OATH OF ALLEGIANCE

I hereby declare, on oath, that I absolutely and entirely renounce and abjure all allegiance and fidelity to any foreign prince, potentate, state, or sovereignty of whom or which I have heretofore been a subject or citizen; that I will support and defend the Constitution and laws of the United States against all enemies, foreign and domestic; that I will bear true faith and allegiance to the same; and that I take this obligation freely without any mental reservation or purpose of evasion: SO HELP ME GOD. In acknowledgment whereof I have hereunto affixed my signature.

Saverio Bernardo Iovino
(Signature of petitioner)

JUL 6 1948

Sworn to in open court, this day of A. D. 19

Clerk.

By Deputy Clerk.

NOTE.—In renunciation of title or order of nobility, add the following to the oath of allegiance before it is signed: "I further renounce the title of (give title or titles) which I have heretofore held," or "I further renounce the order of nobility (give the order of nobility) to which I have heretofore belonged."

Petition granted: Line No. 12 of List No. 7934 and Certificate 6319304 issued.

Petition denied: List No.

Petition continued from to Reason

U. S. GOVERNMENT PRINTING OFFICE c10—16450-1

A GATEWAY TO A NATION ~ An inspiration to the world ~ The Statue of Liberty Museum ~ New York, NY
LibertyEllisFoundation.org/liberty

Printed in the United States
By Bookmasters